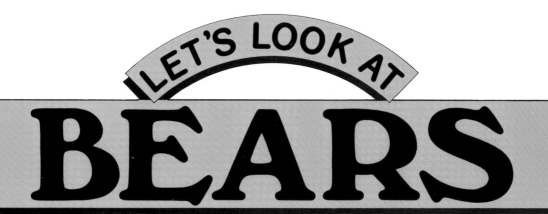

LET'S LOOK AT
BEARS

Malcolm Penny

Language Consultant
Diana Bentley
University of Reading

Artist
David Palmer

The Bookwright Press
New York • 1990

Let's Look at

© Copyright 1989 Wayland (Publishers) Ltd

Library of Congress Cataloging-in-Publication Data
Penny, Malcolm
  Let's look at bears/by Malcolm Penny.
    p. cm. — (Let's look at)
  Bibliography: p.
  Includes index.
    Summary: An introduction to different kinds of bears, their physical characteristics, habits, natural environment, and relationship with people.
    ISBN 0–531–18321–1
    1. Bears—Juvenile literature. [1. Bears.] I. Title.
  II. Series: Let's look at (New York, N.Y.)
  QL763.P46 1990
  599.74'446—dc20   89–7385
                                      CIP
                                      AC

Phototypeset by Kalligraphics, Horley, Surrey
Printed by Casterman, S.A., Belgium

First published in the United States by
The Bookwright Press
387 Park Avenue South,
New York NY 10016

First Published in 1989 by
Wayland (Publishers) Ltd
61 Western Road, Hove
East Sussex BN3 1JD, England

Words printed in **bold** are explained in the glossary.

Contents

What is a bear?

Bears are large furry animals, with short strong legs and long claws. Some bears weigh as much as a cow. They are **mammals**, which means that mother bears produce milk to feed their **cubs**.

All bears have small eyes and little rounded ears. They look rather friendly and cuddly, but they can be quite fierce.

Different kinds of bears

There are seven different kinds of bears in the world. Some bears' names come from their color – like brown bears or black bears. Some are named after the place where they live – like polar bears. Some bears get their names from the markings on their body – like spectacled bears.

Black bear

Sun bear

Spectacled bear

Sloth bear

Grizzly and polar bears are the biggest meat-eating animals on land. Polar bears eat mostly seals. Grizzly bears eat many kinds of food. They eat salmon, young deer, fruit, roots and insect **grubs**.

Polar bear

Grizzly bear

7

Brown bears

Long ago, brown bears lived in
forests all over the northern part of
the world. Then people moved in,
and hunters, farmers and ranchers
killed many bears. Now brown bears
only live where there are not many
people, in wild parts of Canada,
Alaska and the USSR.

   Grizzly bears are a type of brown
bear. They live in parts of North
America.

Brown bears are not really dangerous unless they are hurt or afraid. However, mother bears will fight to save their cubs from danger. It is safer to leave bears alone.

The biggest brown bears are nearly ten feet (three meters) long.

9

Food for brown bears

Brown bears eat all sorts of food. They like berries and fruits, and they dig up roots with their long claws. They dig for small animals like mice, which live in holes in the ground. They will eat baby deer if they can catch them.

In summer, when salmon are swimming up rivers from the sea, the bears go fishing. They jump into the water and catch the salmon with their claws and teeth.

11

Sleepy brown bears

When winter comes, brown bears cannot find any more food. They dig a hole in the side of a hill, and make a bed in it with grass and leaves. Then they lie down and go to sleep until the spring.

In very cold winters when there is a lot of snow, the bears sleep for about five months. They wake up from time to time, but they stay in their **den** until the weather gets warmer. When they come out, they are thin and very hungry.

Baby bears

Baby bears are born during the winter, while the mother is in her den. Brown bears have two or three cubs. When they are born, they are blind and have almost no fur.

By the time spring comes, the little bear cubs will have grown their fur and opened their eyes. Up to now they have been feeding on milk from their mother.

In May, the mother bear leads her cubs out to find food. Soon they learn to catch mice and fish. In the autumn, they will grow fat on berries like their mother. Then they will be ready to sleep through the winter.

15

Mother and cubs

Brown bear cubs stay with their
mother from one and one-half to
over four years. She protects them
from danger while they are small. If
a wolf comes too close, the mother
chases her cubs up a tree, and then
drives the wolf away.

When the cubs grow up, the
females stay near their mother, but
the males move away to find
another place to live.

Black bears

American black bears are smaller than brown bears. They live in forests in North America, especially in **National Parks**, where people come to see the animals.

Black bears often come to **camp-sites** to look for food. Campers have to store their food in metal boxes, which the bears cannot open.

There are bears with black fur in other countries, too, especially in northern India, southern China and Japan. They are sometimes called "moon bears" because they have a round white mark on their chests.

Polar bears

Polar bears live in the **Arctic**, around the North Pole, where there is snow and ice all the year round. The males go on hunting all through the winter for meat, even though it is dark all the time. The females hide away to have their cubs in a den under the snow.

Polar bears hunt seals on the ice, creeping up on them before they can escape into the water. A mother bear with cubs has to eat a seal every day if she is not to go hungry.

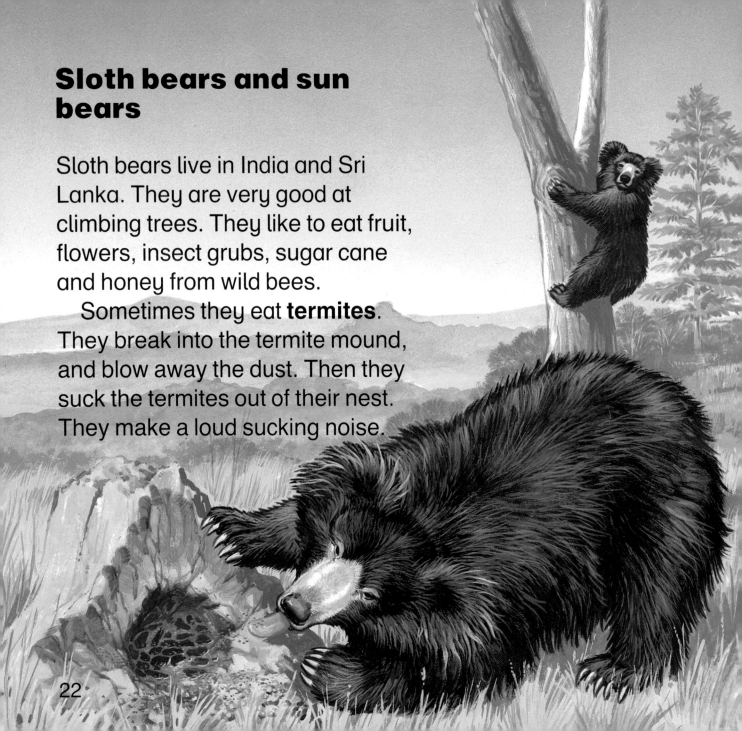

Sloth bears and sun bears

Sloth bears live in India and Sri Lanka. They are very good at climbing trees. They like to eat fruit, flowers, insect grubs, sugar cane and honey from wild bees.

Sometimes they eat **termites**. They break into the termite mound, and blow away the dust. Then they suck the termites out of their nest. They make a loud sucking noise.

Sun bears are the smallest of all bears, not much more than three feet (one meter) long. They live in Southeast Asia. They can climb even better than sloth bears. They can be a nuisance, because they climb coconut palms and **cocoa** trees and steal fruit. Sun bears are also known as "honey bears" because they love honey too!

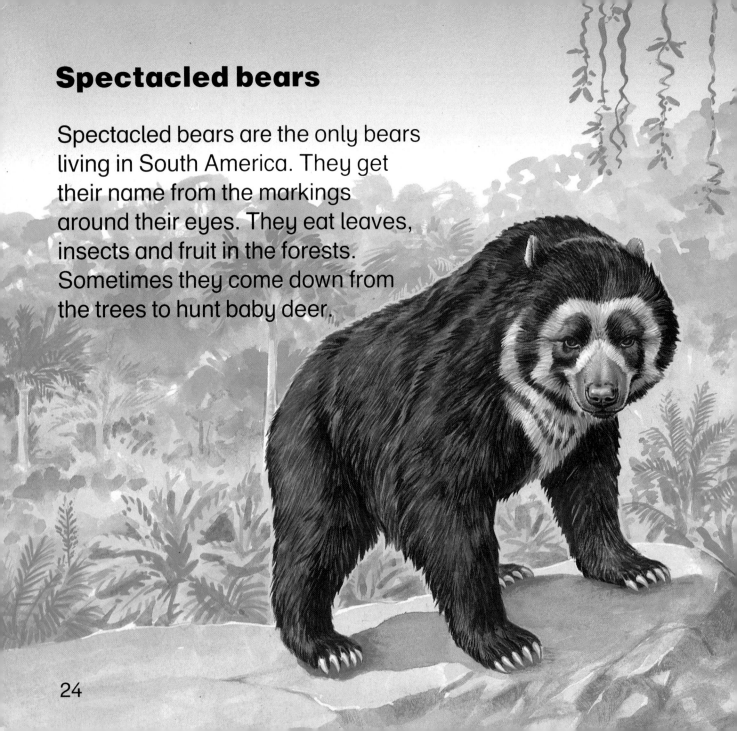

Spectacled bears

Spectacled bears are the only bears living in South America. They get their name from the markings around their eyes. They eat leaves, insects and fruit in the forests. Sometimes they come down from the trees to hunt baby deer.

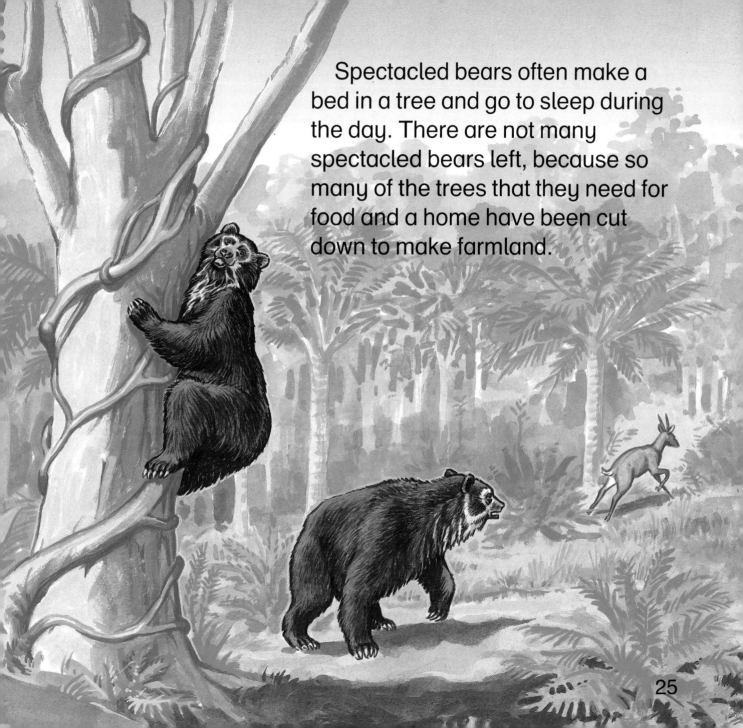

Spectacled bears often make a bed in a tree and go to sleep during the day. There are not many spectacled bears left, because so many of the trees that they need for food and a home have been cut down to make farmland.

25

Not really bears

Giant pandas are not really bears, although they look like them. They are related to the **raccoon** family of animals. They live in the mountains of China. Their only food is **bamboo**. There are now only a few pandas left because they cannot find enough bamboo forests to live in.

Koalas look like bears, too. They live in Australia. A mother koala carries her baby in a **pouch**, like a kangaroo. Koalas eat the leaves of gum trees, which are poisonous to almost all other animals.

Bears and people

Children have had teddy bears as toys for over a hundred years. There are many stories about bears, like *Goldilocks and the Three Bears*, or the stories of Pooh Bear and Paddington Bear. Pooh and Paddington are very friendly bears. People like bears even though they can sometimes be frightening.

Bears are not dangerous if people leave them alone. We should try to make sure that we leave plenty of forests where bears can live happily.

Glossary

Arctic   The part of the world around the North Pole.

Bamboo   A tall grass which can be dried to make canes.

Campsites   Places where people can stay on vacation, in a tent or camper.

Cocoa   A fruit that is used to make chocolate.

Cub   A baby bear.

Den   A place where a bear sleeps during the winter.

Grubs   Baby insects, who have just hatched from their eggs.

Mammals   Animals that are warm-blooded and that produce milk to feed their young.

National Park   An area of land owned by the government, in order to protect its natural beauty and wildlife.

Pouch   A sack-like bag on the tummy of a kangaroo or koala, where its young are carried.

Raccoon   A North American mammal with black stripes on its tail.

Termites   Insects that live in mounds of earth.

Books to read

Bears by Norman Barrett (Franklin Watts, 1988).

A Closer Look at Bears and Pandas, Rev. Edn., by Bobby Whittaker (Gloucester, 1986).

The Black Bear by Mark Ahlstrom (Crestwood House, 1985).

A Closer Look at Arctic Lands, Rev. Edn., by Jill Hughes (Gloucester, 1987).

Pandas by Norman Barrett (Franklin Watts, 1988).

Polar Animals by Norman Barrett (Franklin Watts, 1988).

Seven True Bear Stories by Carol Maistro (Hastings, 1979).

Index